The Asteroid Belt

by Betsy Rathburn

Illustrated by Natalya Karpova

BLASTOFF!

MISSIONS

BELLWETHER MEDIA
MINNEAPOLIS, MN

Blastoff! Missions takes you on a learning adventure! Colorful illustrations and exciting narratives highlight cool facts about our world and beyond. Read the mission goals and follow the narrative to gain knowledge, build reading skills, and have fun!

BLASTOFF!
MISSIONS

Traditional Nonfiction

BLASTOFF! READERS

BLASTOFF! Beginners

BLASTOFF! DISCOVERY

BLASTOFF! MISSIONS

Narrative Nonfiction

Blastoff! Universe

MISSION GOALS

> FIND YOUR SIGHT WORDS IN THE BOOK.

> LEARN ABOUT THE DIFFERENT OBJECTS IN THE ASTEROID BELT.

> FIND SOMETHING IN THE BOOK THAT YOU WOULD LIKE TO LEARN MORE ABOUT.

This edition first published in 2023 by Bellwether Media, Inc.

No part of this publication may be reproduced in whole or in part without written permission of the publisher. For information regarding permission, write to Bellwether Media, Inc., Attention: Permissions Department, 6012 Blue Circle Drive, Minnetonka, MN 55343.

Library of Congress Cataloging-in-Publication Data

Names: Rathburn, Betsy, author.
Title: The asteroid belt / by Betsy Rathburn.
Description: Minneapolis, MN : Bellwether Media, 2023. | Series: Blastoff! missions. Journey into space | Includes bibliographical references and index. | Audience: Ages 5-8 | Audience: Grades 2-3 |
Summary: "Vibrant illustrations accompany information about the asteroid belt. The narrative nonfiction text is intended for students in kindergarten through third grade." -- Provided by publisher.
Identifiers: LCCN 2022006627 (print) | LCCN 2022006628 (ebook) | ISBN 9781644876534 (library binding) | ISBN 9781648348372 (paperback) | ISBN 9781648346996 (ebook)
Subjects: LCSH: Asteroid belt--Juvenile literature. | Asteroids--Juvenile literature.
Classification: LCC QB651 . R38 2023 (print) | LCC QB651 (ebook) | DDC 523.44--dc23/eng/20220228
LC record available at https://lccn.loc.gov/2022006627
LC ebook record available at https://lccn.loc.gov/2022006628

Text copyright © 2023 by Bellwether Media, Inc. BLASTOFF! MISSIONS and associated logos are trademarks and/or registered trademarks of Bellwether Media, Inc.

Editor: Christina Leaf   Designer: Jeffrey Kollock

Printed in the United States of America, North Mankato, MN.

This is **Blastoff Jimmy**! He is here to help you on your mission and share fun facts along the way!

Table of Contents

Journey to the Asteroid Belt

Your class is visiting the science museum.
You learn about the asteroid belt.
This huge, donut-shaped area is far
from Earth. What is it like there?
Your imagination takes you on
a journey to space!

So Many Asteroids

Mars

Wahoo!

You travel past Mars to reach the asteroid belt.

Asteroids stretch in every direction.
They are many miles apart.
You have no trouble weaving
between the rocks as you explore.

asteroid

Some of the asteroids are huge!
Others are smaller than a house.

▶ JIMMY SAYS ◀

All the asteroids put together would be smaller than Earth's moon!

No two asteroids look the same. One looks like a heart. Another looks like a lumpy potato!

You make your way around one of the asteroids. It looks like a dark lump of clay. A similar asteroid passes nearby. There must be thousands of them!

S-type asteroid

M-type asteroid

Suddenly, an asteroid swooshes past you. It is bright and shiny, catching light from the Sun. It looks like it is made of metal!

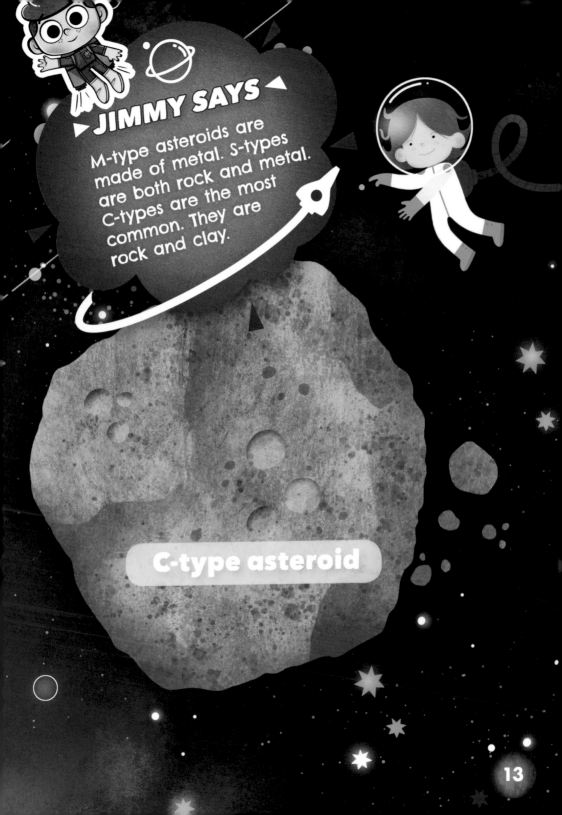

▶JIMMY SAYS ◀

M-type asteroids are made of metal. S-types are both rock and metal. C-types are the most common. They are rock and clay.

C-type asteroid

The Biggest Asteroids

Vesta

You head deeper into the asteroid belt. You want to explore some of the biggest objects. Vesta is nearby. It is the biggest asteroid in the belt!

As you continue around the belt, an even larger object **looms**. It is bigger and rounder than any asteroid. It is the **dwarf planet** Ceres!

You fly closer to peek into its many **craters**.

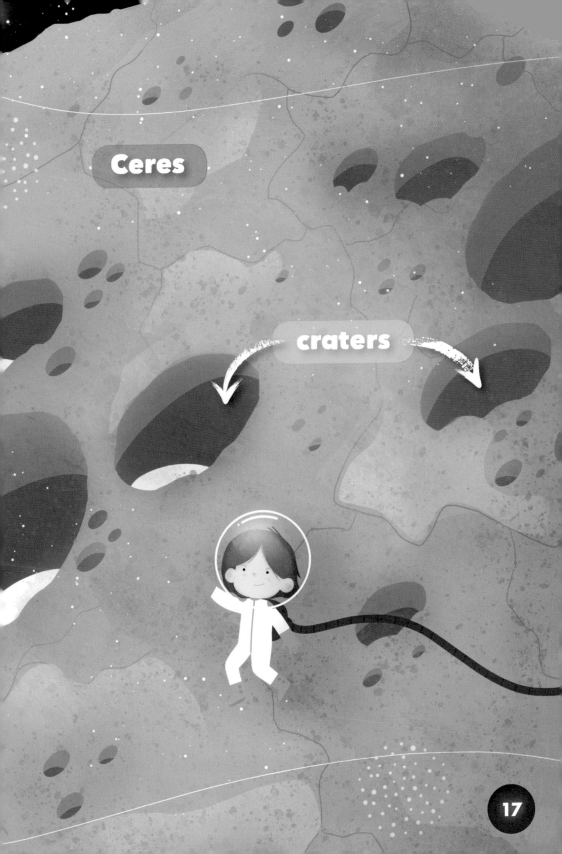

Ceres

craters

At the outer edge of the asteroid belt, something blasts past you.

Nearby Jupiter's **gravity** knocked an asteroid out of **orbit**. You hope it stays far from Earth!

Jupiter

It is time to head back to Earth. In the museum, you find yourself alone. Your class has moved on. Better catch up!

Asteroid Belt Objects

Ceres

How to say it: SEAR-ees

Asteroid Belt Size Rank: 1

Type: dwarf planet

Vesta

How to say it: VEST-ah

Asteroid Belt Size Rank: 2

Type: asteroid

Pallas

How to say it: PAL-us

Asteroid Belt Size Rank: 3

Type: asteroid

Hygiea

How to say it: hi-JEE-uh

Asteroid Belt Size Rank: 4

Type: asteroid

Glossary

craters–holes in the surface of an object

dwarf planet–a space object that looks like a small planet

gravity–a force that pulls objects toward each other

looms–appears in the distance

orbit–a fixed path around something

To Learn More

AT THE LIBRARY

Kurtz, Kevin. *Comets and Asteroids in Action: An Augmented Reality Experience*. Minneapolis, Minn.: Lerner Publications, 2020.

London, Martha. *Explore Asteroids*. Minneapolis, Minn.: Abdo, 2021.

Rathburn, Betsy. *The Dwarf Planets*. Minneapolis, Minn.: Bellwether Media, 2023.

ON THE WEB

FACTSURFER

Factsurfer.com gives you a safe, fun way to find more information.

1. Go to www.factsurfer.com.

2. Enter "asteroid belt" into the search box and click 🔍.

3. Select your book cover to see a list of related content.

BEYOND THE MISSION

> WHAT FACT FROM THE BOOK DID YOU THINK WAS MOST INTERESTING?

> MAKE YOUR OWN ASTEROIDS FROM MATERIALS AROUND YOUR HOME.

> MAKE UP AN ASTEROID. WHAT IS ITS NAME? WHAT DOES IT LOOK LIKE?

Index